TEACUPS AND TEDDY BEARS

by

John D. Dydo

This book was written in the loving memory of my beautiful Godmother/Auntie Donna and unfiltered, outspoken Gramma Marie. It is dedicated to my loving Mom, Mary, inspiring cousin Stella, and Andrea, the sister I had literally wished for as a little boy. Their unwavering support has and will always be my saving grace.

The contents of this work, including, but not limited to, the accuracy of events, people, and places depicted; opinions expressed; permission to use previously published materials included; and any advice given or actions advocated are solely the responsibility of the author, who assumes all liability for said work and indemnifies the publisher against any claims stemming from publication of the work.

All Rights Reserved
Copyright © 2024 by John D. Dydo

No part of this book may be reproduced or transmitted, downloaded, distributed, reverse engineered, or stored in or introduced into any information storage and retrieval system, in any form or by any means, including photocopying and recording, whether electronic or mechanical, now known or hereinafter invented without permission in writing from the publisher.

Dorrance Publishing Co
585 Alpha Drive
Suite 103
Pittsburgh, PA 15238
Visit our website at www.dorrancebookstore.com

ISBN: 979-8-89211-020-4
eISBN: 979-8-89211-518-6

Johnny was a boy—a very special boy.
He wasn't like the other boys who played catch and rumble fumble.
Some of Johnny's favorite things to do were playing house with his stuffed animals, dressing up and making believe.

Johnny loved his whole family, but most especially the ladies.

He loved his mom with all his heart, but not so much when she got sad.

He loved his gramma. She took the time to show him how to do things—like cooking and baking.

He loved his cousin Stella. She was an artist who painted pretty pictures.

But he particularly loved his Auntie Donna, who also happened to be his godmother. She always made him feel like the best little boy in the world.

Johnny also loved movies. His favorite was about a little girl and her dog trying to find their way home. They were being chased by a wicked witch. The witch scared and excited Johnny all at the same time.

Johnny's favorite time of the year happened to be Halloween. It was the only time that he could dress up and not be scolded.

This Halloween would be different because this year he was in kindergarten, and there was a going to be a costume parade.

Johnny thought long and hard about his costume. He really wanted to be the wicked witch. He was very excited by the possibility. So, he snuck into his parent's bedroom, and rubbed all kinds of make up on his face trying to match the witch's scary green one.

His mother walked in and she was horrified. When she asked him what he was doing, he explained that he wanted to be a witch. She responded, "Absolutely not!"

"Your father and I discussed it. Boys aren't witches. That's a girl's costume. End of story," his mother shrieked.

So he went to his grandma, and she said, "Why don't you be a pizza man? I'll put flour on your cheeks and give you some bread dough to play with."

Disappointed, he then went to his cousin Stella. She laughed, gave him a necklace of colorful beads and kissed him on the forehead.

Finally, he went to his Auntie Donna and explained his problem. She answered, "You can be anything you dream of, that's what Halloween is all about."
"But my mom won't even get me a cheap plastic witch costume from the dollar store," he replied. Auntie responded, "If you wish hard enough anything is possible."

The next day was Halloween and Johnny sadly packed his backpack with his big brother's old cowboy costume.

Later that afternoon when it was time to put on his costume, Johnny couldn't find his backpack.

His teacher then called him aside because he had a special visitor. He turned around and saw a lady dressed all in pink and gold with two tiny wings on her back. She was carrying a bright orange jack-o'-lantern brimming with flowing black material.

The fairy lady whisked him into the coat closet and transformed him in minutes.

When he stepped out in full green face, a black wig and a pointed hat, he made the best little witch ever. The whole room clapped loudly and cheered.

He ran back to the coat closet, but the fairy lady was gone. And instead, Auntie Donna was standing there with open arms.

She bent down and whispered, "Sometimes wishes do come true especially if you have a fairy godmother."

Printed in the USA
CPSIA information can be obtained
at www.ICGtesting.com
LVHW070932171024
793465LV00025B/167